The Sanity of Earth and Grass

COMPLETE POEMS

ROBERT WINNER

Selected and edited by Jane Cooper,
Thomas Lux, and Sylvia Winner

*With forewords by Thomas Lux
and Jane Cooper*

Tilbury House, Publishers
Gardiner, Maine

Tilbury House, Publishers
132 Water Street
Gardiner, Maine 04345

First printing.

Library of Congress Cataloging-in-Publication Data

Winner, Robert, 1930-1986
      The sanity of earth and grass : complete poems / by Robert Winner;
      selected and edited by Jane Cooper, Thomas Lux, and Sylvia Winner;
      with forewords by Thomas Lux and Jane Cooper.
          p.   cm.
      ISBN: 0-88448-140-9 : $12.95 ISBN: 0-88448-139-5 : $19.95
      I. Cooper, Jane, 1924-   . II. Lux, Thomas, 1946-   .
   III. Winner, Sylvia, 1926-   . IV. Title.
PS3573.I5323A17   1994
811' .54--dc20
                                                           93-37897
                                                              CIP

This book is dedicated
to Bob's devoted friends

No words can express my gratitude to Jane
Cooper and Thomas Lux for their constant
encouragement and tireless efforts in working
with me to prepare this book.
—Sylvia Winner

Contents

Green in the Body (1979)

I

II

III

Flogging the Czar (1983)

I

II

III

IV

Foreword by Thomas Lux

When I first met Robert Winner in the early fall of 1977, I knew
he was a man I would come to love. He was then 47, sixteen years
my senior, and I was immediately struck by the force of his charac-
ter — both in the poems he showed me and in his presence.

At that time, Bob was a part-time student in the fledgling
Master of Fine Arts program at Sarah Lawrence College, where I
was teaching. He had come to my office to discuss the possibility
of working with me in a conference course, a one-on-one tutorial
in poetry writing. That was the first of a hundred or so meetings,
which continued long after our official term ended. Often we
would meet in restaurants in New York City — first-floor spaces
where his wheelchair could easily go. On rare occasions, he even
allowed me to pick up the check! We'd have lunch, sometimes
dinner, and talk about poetry for a few hours.

Early in our friendship, he told me that after his spinal cord
injury in a diving accident at age sixteen, he determined to do two
things in his life. One was to become financially independent
(being a quadriplegic was, and is, appallingly expensive) and the
other was to marry. He managed the first by being very smart at
business. And he married Sylvia in 1969. They had been together
for more than seventeen years when Bob died in 1986, and let me
put it down here: never have I known a man so deeply, consis-
tently, and sanely in love. Bob was also a devoted stepfather to
Sylvia's daughter Lisa, who was seventeen (he began his parenting
with a teenager!) at the time of the wedding.

If asked to define the central aesthetic of Robert Winner's
poetry, I would say it was a dedication to absolute clarity and
honesty. He had neither time for nor interest in the opaque,
oblique, fuzzy, or decorative qualities of so much verse. Joy,
celebration, sometimes lamentation (though never lugubrious),

true mystery or pure wonder, and an unending and unconquerable passion for living — these were the things that did interest him and informed his work. There was some darkness too, but never nihilistic cynicism, or coldness, or self-pity. In poem after poem we hear a real human being speaking to other real human beings — unafraid of emotion, risking sentimentality but rarely falling prey to it.

Do not let the apparent simplicity of these poems fool you. Part of Bob's art lay in making artifice disappear. He was his own painstaking editor, a relentless reviser, crafting draft after draft of every poem. In the thirty-one previously uncollected poems that we (Sylvia Winner, Jane Cooper, and myself) pulled from note-books and piles of unpublished typescript, we often had a difficult time deciding which version to use. We chose these poems, even though Bob probably did not consider them finished, because they seemed to us, nevertheless, whole.

All of these whole poems, in fact, come from a man who was whole, a man who I was privileged to have as a friend, and who has become for me an indispensable poet. And now it is a privilege to have this book, this beautiful, tender, fierce, and deeply human book.

Foreword by Jane Cooper

When I think of how, and for how long, I knew Robert Winner, I
first come up with snapshots: Bob being wheeled around the Sarah
Lawrence campus while he was still an undergraduate — hand-
some, healthy, radiantly intelligent face. (I assumed he was a
World War II veteran, like his friend at the controls.) Then, Bob
and Sylvia by the brook at his summer place in Putnam Valley,
before they were married, talking. When did we first start look-
ing at poems together? That is irrecoverable, but I remember
reading an early draft of "Wall Street," over dinner in their New
York City apartment with Bob and Sylvia, married now, and Helen
Lynd, and how elated we all were. Next, Bob in an adamant and
even quite thunderous mood as he insisted he should enter Sarah
Lawrence's new graduate program in writing; I was arguing —
fruitlessly, of course — that as a poet he was already way past the
level at which we could teach him anything. Finally, Bob at
Sylvia's sixtieth birthday party, tired, proud, profoundly satisfied,
only a few evenings before his sudden death.

One stubborn truth of Bob Winner's existence was that he spent
forty years in a wheelchair, from 1946 to the end. Somehow I
always want to add that statistic to "The Ruler," a poem of his full
poetic maturity. Not only did he confound all the doctors' predic-
tions, but he lived longer as a quadriplegic that anyone else of his
generation with his particular kind of spinal cord injury. Yet this
fact was never allowed into the biographical matter in either of his
books. Instead, his nineteen years as a stockbroker, his presidency
of a small but demanding family company, the names of magazines
that had printed his poems were scrupulously chronicled. He
never wanted special treatment. Though some poems, notably in
his second collection, *Flogging the Czar*, were frank about the
paralysis and about his anger and grief, he wanted them to

command respect *as poems*, and they did, and do. Still it's my hope that, by speaking of his disability now, his editors can point not only to the heroism of the work but to its usefulness, as an exercise of the spirit.

Let it be said at the same time how funny Bob was — and, as Sylvia is quick to add, never at anyone's expense, "not even his own." She once made a list of his passions: travel, Shakespeare, sex, poetry, music, delicious food, the sun — "not necessarily in that order." Furthermore, he truly enjoyed business, at which he was very good; he loved machines and could be (through his chauffeur, at whom he fired orders) a breath-stopping driver; he was a voracious reader of books of all sorts. Place Wallace Stevens next to Shakespeare and Mozart in his pantheon, that meditative, musical, outrageously inventive genius who once walked from New York City all the way home to Hartford. Vital energy in all its forms appealed to Bob, and it was the secret of his poems.

Thomas Lux has already written well concerning those poems, so I will just say that what I valued most during Bob's lifetime was his combination of hard truthfulness with delight in the earth, the "enormous kindness of sensation." Hurrah for any poet who can announce, "What I like is smell"! At the same time, I watched as Bob slowly gained the power and spareness to incorporate into his poems the "price of Experience," to move from work on the poem-as-artifact to the far more difficult and life-consuming (life-enhancing) task of writing what had so far seemed out of bounds. "Learning To Mourn," for instance, which was originally part of his first book, I remember as a watershed poem. He adored the natural world, but he never forgot how and where most of us lead our lives. There was his determined democracy, so different from anything to be found in Stevens.

A word is in order here concerning the shape of this book. Once we had made our selection of previously unpublished poems, we had to decide how true to be to chronology. But since five significant poems from *Green in the Body* had already been reprinted, some in slightly different form, in *Flogging the Czar*, it was in any case impossible to present Bob's first book as it had appeared. Accordingly, the remaining *Green in the Body* poems, together with three early unpublished ones, became Section II. Twenty-eight later unpublished works, under the title Bob had tentatively selected for his third book, *The Health of the World*, became Section I. While it is our conviction that all these poems are good and some are among Bob's very best, how he would have arranged them, what changes he would still have made, and above all what he would have added, are among the mysteries. *Flogging the Czar* is given intact as Section III, because as a sustained composition it seems the most complete evidence of Bob's artistry.

I was once told that the old emperors of China, wanting to register admiration for a favorite scroll painting, would often simply copy out the words of a previous prince or poet. So — what a privilege it is for all of us to have this book, this "beautiful, tender, fierce, and deeply human book."

The Sanity of
Earth and Grass

The Health of the World

> *It seems*
> *As if the health of the world might be enough.*
> *It seems as if the honey of common summer*
> *Might be enough, . . .*
> *As if pain, no longer satanic mimicry,*
> *Could be borne, as if we were sure to find our way.*

—Wallace Stevens: "Esthétique du Mal"

Land's End

Surviving in its fragile skin,
a white egret rises
from the gulf of its strength.
I want the lightest needle of a pine
to fall on my hand,
a pine with ravaged limbs.

I'd stare through salt-blind eyes
at a remote fragile sea. I'd roar.
I'd make the skeleton of grief.
I'd roar like you, unreconciled sea.

Concentration Camp Numbers

Under the graft of thigh skin
the numbers darken the lymph-melt:
inked mementos of corpses,
of blood on the face from beatings,
rooted as the memories of fingers
in the stump of a hand.

It's pain that teaches you your real identity:
your own skull facing you on the table.

Let me know this God of apples,
roses, worms, and frozen rivers:
let me know the worst conceived by Him.
I'd say: Come on!
I'd like to know that misty conception,
an unmarked life.

Daybreak

Flat on my bed
enjoying the very idea of flatness
the beauty of weight
as if I were the horizon. . .
Daylight comes slow
mounting alterations on the wall.
Sun, you come back, filling your place.

What a thing it is to have this power,
to climb to the very tip of daylight.

The Health of the World

Sands had been on a hunger strike since May 1st, demanding political prisoner privileges. . . for himself and the other IRA convicts at the Maze (Prison). At week's end Sands weighed less than 100 lbs., and was by his own enfeebled estimation: "days from death."

—*Time* Magazine, May 4, 1981

It seems as if the health of the world might be enough. . .

—Wallace Stevens

I lie in a hospital room, post-surgery,
Straining to gain myself back
From helplessness, not quite believing
I'll make it, not quite believing
The news on television at my bedpost:
Bearded, jail-white faces of young men
Starving themselves,

Starving themselves for the word *political*
In shit-smeared jail cells—hunger strikers
Wrapped in blankets, wincing at camera lights. . .
I want this life they throw away.
I want their health, even the dregs of it.
I want what's left of the heartbeats
Of Bobby Sands, his life's slow-
Motion stumbling bludgeoned by his will.

Something insignificant—
An earthworm or snail inside my body—
Wants me to live. Something ordinary—
My boyhood Bronx neighborhood, mostly Irish,
With its immigrant brogues and Lenten ashes,
Its raw wintry faces and granite church—
Wants me to praise those obscure lives.

Something foolhardy in me also,
Something I dreamed once: infiltrating
Hitler's Germany to save Jews
Filled with power by the word *Jew*,
Always afraid I'd be given away by blunders,
Caught red-handed in my own dream,

Something that longs to stand upright—
As in this hospital, squirming
Away from death, I long to occupy
That human reckless unbalanced perpendicular—
Makes me feel what everyone feels:
The mystery of their gesture, these jailbirds
Laying down their lives for so much
Sweet death, given the right song.

Siberia

The way your life turns out
Opposite to your expectations. . .
The fingerprints of days erased,
Snowflakes, chess games on long nights. . .
What you've lived you've lived alone
Once and for all time
In the company of the earth.

Verdi

Verdi was popular in his lifetime;
a big success
although spurned by the Conservatory.
His wife and children died within two years.
Verdi was beside himself,
but stuck to business.
He sang.

That dogged lyricism—
no one needs to know how it happened.
He threw into his black-inked scores
his father's hoe, his mother's stove,
his own thick organist's fingers,
the green and ochre of Parma's plain,
Italian summers, crafty Italian winters,
the freedom Italy longed for.

Verdi wowing us at the opera,
Verdi brought in with the wine,
Verdi summoning with an overture
in cracked brass—evenings
in thousands of piazzas.

Still Life

I think of my father
Working quietly at an easel,
With small strokes globing
The fruit and wine bottles.
How many breasts he painted
In pears and oranges and green glass,
Getting inside the blouses of things
Twice a week in the rented studio
He shared downtown.
The stillness of the subjects,
And their reticence, appealed to him.
They didn't risk too much
Emotion, like this poem,
Because, after all, we can cry for our dead
Too much: perhaps they remain as apples,
Fish on platters, bottles of red wine. . .

Rush Hour

The need to pull over, to stop,
To escape the groaning highway,
To gaze at trees, the pylons
Of a high-tension powerline,
And the smoke-stained sunset
Against which they're poised, skeletal—
To join their world, to hear
The words of their communion,
To go nowhere like things,

Like skeletons, like the traveling
American Tobacco salesman I once met
Parked along a mountain road,
Staring at rapids—a stream's
White-flecked scrambling over rocks,
To stop near him and watch the water
That rushed on and on yet remained there,
To commune, heads bent, to loosen
Our white shirts and neckties,
To be soothed down our spines
By that soft thunder, that spell.

The Trouble with Icarus

The trouble was the smile of Daedalus,
a condescension so stupendous
it made the boy wince to think about himself.
It made him kneel
and break little things he tried to fix.

So that when freedom opened both its arms,
when they flew from Crete,
he wanted to fly embellishments.
He wanted to loop and dive
in circles round the overconfident old man,
rowing as steadily as breath.

The sea two miles below, hammered metal.

He wanted to touch that stony heart with admiration,
to get some gesture of respect.
He felt he could touch the sun
and not be harmed.

Cockcrow

If we could gather up our meaning,
stand in the sun's mindless light,
crack ourselves open, run the risks
and repeat the terrifying howl of the obvious

to find what goes without saying,
cries that give the sun back
to the world of the sun,
all soft phantoms of obscurity gone,

the heart would waken in dangerous brilliance,
bellows of courage tuned to major,
stone of equal determination
taking the sun to its vastest height.

Seed

This puny capsule
nuzzling earth. . .
to be eaten, or rot with damp

or breaking out
of its shell, spill
its thunder of ideas on the world.

Sickroom

I try to carry the gravestone
from the darkness of my mother's sickroom—
scratches of light around drawn shades—
outside, the gold and red of autumn.

She is like a queen in exile
scraping with her nails on silk walls
her message of anger, her weak
insatiable demands and regrets.

I want her to grow rosy old
like a maple leaf, ripening,
yielding only to that ice edged wind that must come
and cut her down—like me, like everyone.

Jahrzeit

In her first breakdown, Mother
Leaned against you, twisted
Towards you on your dogged walks.
Nothing existed but suffering.
You leaned against the wind.

Now, missing you, I imagine you
Striding buoyantly around the corner,
Blue-eyed, with a deadpan humor,
A good-looking Buster Keaton
On whose face your life really depended.

That granite mask of yours
Saved you many times. Amazed, half-
Smiling at our continuity, I put on
One of your faded shirts.

"Archduke" Trio, Op. 97

Listening to the "Archduke,"
I see the gray man Beethoven
Walking in his woolen sadness
Through the slums and cake-shop jollity
of Vienna, past its palaces. . .

And I know I can sing without reference
To the slums of my own life,
Dreaming up sounds inside a deaf cloud,
As he did, to reach some interior
Happiness of tones, as he did.

Premonition

I was not in safety, neither had I rest, neither was I quiet, yet trouble came.

—*Job* 3, 25-26

My face on someone else's body
smiles from a wheelchair
in the glossy bulletin from
Beth Abraham Home for Incurables.
I'm sixteen like him, baffled—
his hair combed the same preoccupied way—
how can he live like that and smile
(even this weak upward twist of his lips
cajoled by the photographer)?

I know nothing yet about the consequence
of striking, neck-breaking hard,
the sandy bottom of the Little Pigeon River,
East Tennessee.
Like Job's three comforters, I know nothing
about the difficulty of understanding
anyone else's position,
or that I can see myself that moment
in my own future, as I shortly would be,
pinned down flat in *Life, Life's* smile on my face
in a "photographic essay" on the incurable.

18

I was not in safety.
I put the photograph of my double
down, I think forever,
going out to look for birds in the woods,
green myself that day, green as God
before the experience of suffering.

I was not in safety, neither had I rest.
It was a cry I couldn't hear,
an outburst of crouched grief
at what could not be undone,
a darkness shoving daylight aside
to howl at God for making
my unlucky double in a magazine
constantly glide down a corridor
towards me, wearing my face—
crashing into me every time
but noiselessly,
with the impact of shadow.

Passing the Spot

I pass the spot where I almost died
in a car crash; it happened fast—
a stick turned into a snake.

Our arms and hands pulled us out of it,
our body cells wanting to live
while our minds' dumb generals
slept at headquarters.

How easy it was to meet and talk with her—
the other driver, our sideswiped cars
askew at the roadside, moored in grass.
It was gentle, intimate:
we were brother and sister

conspiring against dying.
The heart took a deeper breath.
We knew ourselves one
with the sparrows and flies,

and the red-haired trooper
who wrote our information in his notebook.
The trees looked new, and her face
I was almost in love with:
young, incredibly interesting.

Home

My heart and my bones wince.
It's so damn sad-looking
and ugly, the Bronx—
driving past those small hills
blighted for miles with bleak
six-story desert-alike apartment
buildings—the landscape I come from.
It's so damn ugly in its torment
of knifings and fires, I forget
I was happy there sometimes
in its damp and dingy streets, living my life
with the five continents of the world
in my mind's eye.

Maybe it was beautiful before us:
the coast with no landfill
a bluffed peninsula of swamps and forests,
a wilderness that became another wilderness
—beds and linoleum, school books,
musty hallways, laughter, despondency—
unremembering earth, a riverbed
millions flowed on, clinging briefly
to some masonry, then gone. . .

I come from there, no landscape
to come from, no real hometown
with leaves and porches, drugstore and gas station,
no anchor in green, like Yorkshire

for Captain James Cook. I can imagine him
returning home after circumnavigating
the globe, the South Pacific claimed,
climbing the moors to find
his dreaming stone, his first South Seas
in that sea of wind-blunted grass
and near-emptiness.

But it's the Bronx I come from,
the landscape of hearts, the Bronx
that's washed away continually,
the spirit and flesh that pass through
subways and doorways.
I come from there like the bus driver
who, years ago, tried to escape Gun Hill Road
in his red and yellow transit bus
and was found, days later, in Hollywood,
Florida, a girl on each arm
savoring the fruits of his glory
in the subtropical sunshine, like Captain Cook.

Times Square

On Broadway,
we want the impossible.
That's why it has to be there,
glittering
at the center of town.

We seek out wonders: the flashiest
come-ons, the rooms where
we are altogether ourselves
and altogether accepted

and find a fly-blown theater
frayed and stinking,
and women caked with make-up—
in short, the ordinary world.

But it remains there idealized,
Broadway. If we're lucky
it lasts a lifetime, it speaks
of places where we first learned
dreams enlarged us,
gave us kingdoms of pleasure—

before the turned-down denying mouth
of the other reality—the father
waiting, belt in hand
at the top of stairs—

or con men, pimps and chiselers
got hold of us. . .

Here in this neon heart, among
hookers, panhandlers, out-of-town buyers,
young kids lying about their age,
—in the most unsuspecting, the poorest
in prospects—behind all these faces
reaching for an absolute, I've seen
these billboards garish with happiness,
this stubborn idealism.

Caribbean

Sun, soft and gold. Late afternoon.
A waiter folds napkins
In the glass-enclosed dining room.
His head is down. I can't see his eyes.
Under the satin of my holiday
The clay of his life.

South Bronx

They say the Bedouins have no games,
only feuds. I believe it.

Recovery Room

My name stands next to me,
calling to me: "Wake up!"
The glare of bright lamps
pecks at my eyes. I hear
the gossip of nurses—one nurse
cheerfully taking orders
for coffee and sandwiches.

Days later, alone in my room,
I think how the insect wings
of nerves swarmed over me,
how I risked my life each day
to climb on top of a pile
of handshakes and smiles,
how I walked all over my body
with the jackboots of my longings.

My kidneys, patient as waterwheels,
had no use for these ambitions.
All they wanted was to feel
the leisure of water, the calm
slow turning of day and night.
With tubes in my arms in a white bed
my only longing is to live.

Looking out of the window, I see time
as clouds slow moving over the walls
of houses, through vaults of sky.

I feel myself a multimillionaire of time,
a Daniel Boone in a wilderness
of fatherly trees, who stands on peaks
and sweeps the green horizon with his eyes,
the stonecrop clearings lost in the quiet
of grass—the long foundation of the animals,
holy automatons, ignorant of my need
to volunteer for death.

Flies

Why should flies thrive
Feasting on famine's children,
On soft African eyelids,
And the bureaucrats inflate,
And the police and the black marketeers
Amplify, and the army blossom?
Why should maggots feed so well
And the people shrivel,
Skulls in the sand?

Let these death's-heads howl at God,
They have the right to do it—
Marx, in his museum chair, would weep.
Ideas fly over like ibis, alien to this
Plain of dearth between lakes and marshes
Where the stilted birds set down
Their feet and walk
Elegantly.

Thanksgiving Day, 1983

(On the decision to deploy Pershing II missiles in Europe)

All day rain beats like the war
On everyone's doorstep, the war
That will have no location, no *theatres;*
Two weeks that nobody will remember
Settling the matter like a judge with one arm
Pounding out irreversible sentences.
Yet we eat and are at peace together.
The giant leech of tropical forests
Contents its appetite on nests of worms.
The armed horsemen of the Elgin Marbles
Complete their ride; they end their long
Imprisonment in art and order,
Reach their enemies finally and slake
Their bloodthirst and are themselves
Slaughtered.

Mayday on This Planet of Grass

A chain saw's crazed snarl.
The sounds of cars like surf.
The long acid drone of a Sunday airplane.

This is the revolution
of the flywheel and manic cylinders—
the wings of fern and tree ghosts
hover, uprooted,
blunder into the light,
bearing their own deaths with them.

A few lines from his journal, 1983

I study the alphabet of your skin

    *

The flash of thighs

    *

The intricate rage of games

    *

You take the groan from my throat
and carry it off somewhere
and bury it

    *

Great blocks of silence in the woods
armfuls

    *

Big dance of the ocean, ships like bright July

    *

Car wheels' rubber anguish

*

Death can move in all directions
like the queen in chess

*

The river never arrives on time

*

Called out by the sun
which makes
no demands on us

The River and the Rocks Have Never Tried To Have a Good Time

Even when at night with you
I surround myself with touch,
That dark dark sense,

Like a released convict
Dazed a little, needing time
Outside the prison gate
To grasp his liberty,

I can barely grasp it:
The life of roots and blood,
The fabulous country of the blind.

Water

Four days after her son's death
I was amazed at the firmness
of her voice. I thought
it would have screamed into splinters.

When I mentioned her courage,
tears broke—
a sob she caught
like a falling vase.

She said: I've borne many terrible things
but this is the hardest.
We thought of his life—the competitive furor
of his executive's job,
his four- and five-year-old boys, his divorce.

That night, at the movies, African dancers
thin-legged and supple as water birds
were telling stories of their lives
with limbs and torsos—bodies that sang
like water,
ponds and lakes and rivers and waterfalls,
steady-rhythmed, fountains of brown communion. . .
I thought how fragile we are, how it runs away.

Not made of iron, more like water,
I threw off the clothing of grief

and joined them, carried by the drums
and the stories I didn't know until then
I had to tell.

Bitter Song

The birds are fortunate.
They sing without evasions.
I concentrate like stone
all deaths in the world.

I will go wild in the forest,
a dog dumb with cruelty, the night
against my sides like leaves;
lapping water, the stream's
green stones unmoved
by my lips and tongue.

Green in the Body

Ah! Douce campagna, honey in the heart
Green in the body, out of a petty phrase,
Out of a thing believed, a thing affirmed. . .

—Wallace Stevens: "The Well Dressed Man with a Beard"

I

Horses

I look across some ragged meadows
where I played in summers years before.
Over the neighbor's fence, three horses—
two chestnuts and a dappled gray.
They have been free all night
without a scrap of leather on them,
grazing, huddling close, or moving lazily about.
They seem to have the world to themselves.

I stay there watching them, as if I could eat grass.
The trees are working, they work like stones,
and the horses are a game of childhood,
they are half-ton butterflies.
This meadow is the universe
and I could walk and walk and never reach those horses
always before my eyes the smile of their glossy coats
in the summer sun, the thick grass wet and ripe.

I have walked in the wrong direction all my life,
balancing on railroad tracks away
from anything I could love as well
as that supple ground, that tangled knee-deep grass,
those horses waiting in the expectant distance
watching me come with my wet knees pocked with burrs,
my bridles and my daylight mysteries,
to place my hands against their springy necks,
to feel their strange obedience,
and take my boyhood in my hands again.

Buzzard

In a roofless quiet,
floating on bits of wind,
its great flat wings
thrust out
from its entrails.

To fly is lovely. . .
it is the prince of ugliness,
its crooked head points down,
a finger carving toneless rings
in a blue eye-world.

Deserted Farm

The broken walls remain,
smothered by scrawled weeds,
sumac, prodigal flights of vines
over stones and windows.

I press my fingers down
on grass that was once
part of a dooryard,
or someone's shadow,
and feel it tremble,
escape.

For the grass might be anyone, a boy
who felt the first touch of desire
and turned away.

Goldenrod

I meet in the morning
the dauntless spinster, quick-smiled,
leather-skinned, flat-shoed,
and friendly as the tree her dog waters.

Always cheerful to me and strangers
I don't know her kitchen mind
her closet mood
her cornered evenings facing darkness.

She comes from the country where goldenrod
commandeers meadows in September,
hailing its own tall yellow over the spent grass,
spilling its pollen like sunlight—
and who cares which of the bright tough flowers
breeds the field again?

Spring

Laughter leaps up out of the dead park,
an old black woman's laughter
bearing the dawn of trees
the unexpected self.

Eden

The earth has never needed us.
At an abandoned railway station
small bleached buildings
kneel before the sun. Serene,
they have no more battles to fight
against light and cold.

All the sadness of walls forgotten—
drifting back to earth, disengaged
from the triumph of billboards and schedules,
the rushing arroyos of sweat,
the cracking bones against starvation.
Weeds bury the rails'
four rusty teeth laid out
along the river's mercury slab.

High in their winds, the hoodlum gulls
glide down to sunlit water, like ideas
descending to reality. In mounds of leaves
squirrels and mice forage
in their morose routines, all of them
breathing a cry of life
with the whole world Sunday—
an everyday like the animals' hunger.

9 to 5

How can the wind find me—
on this street, caught between
disciplined walls of office buildings,
windows of fish silence,
stratagems of hunger behind glass?

How can it slam against my body,
tear around me, surprise me—
diving among walls to touch my face—
bearing its dust, its swill-thick river smells—
surround me with the forest's privacy,
the sanity of earth and grass,
the sea stretched out beside this island
like the fin of sleep?

To My Face, After Illness

From your bones on out
you give the lie to suffering.
You ought to be more lined with pain.
You should make a stronger impression
in photographs
of the heartbreak caged in your fat.

Mess of tissues!
Maybe I should be grateful to you
for remembering,
for leaving printed on this flesh—
its sun-tanned jowls—
those inescapable paragraphs
which tell the original story.

Stone in August

Sun-whitened, sprawled in deep grass,
small reflections laced with quartz and iron,
a continent's milk compressed.

Sweet ship of summer floating in the field
all banners blowing in the heat burned into you
plunged in some vital silence of your own
that even to the wind is central.

Quietness made before mind, sustained,
the years flow into you and you hold them
without decay, bone of the intangible.

Red of fish and vulture's white
snake's blue and the clouds—
the summer's gladness of your being
heaved from the earth,

I would dance on you, stone.
I would make more life of you.

A War

The green marsh wakens with birds at dusk
from the afternoon sleep of cattails—
sandpipers wading on thin bent legs,
sparrows clinging to reeds,
and herons stalking somewhere in small channels.

It gives me joy to know them, near
to my great walks out of boyhood, to feel
the rancid breath of wilderness touch my face
the stride in front of me,
the world in front of my shoes.

Just behind me, the highway. Traffic, blazing
islands of gas pumps, fast-food joints—
a screen of light against the darkening sky.

I watch some killdeer peck at the rubbled margins,
tasting our swill in their swamp food.
They hop among three yellow bulldozers
parked haphazardly for the night.
How strange and brave they are to come,
fighting for their small lives almost in secret.

Penguins

In the long months between nestings
in the fierce Antarctica,
no one has ever found them.
They disappear as we do under faces and clothes.
I laugh at the way they stand up straight,
at the flapping of their atrophied wings.
I have seen one die in a seal's mouth—
ripped to skeleton and beak and floating blood
in a matter of thirty seconds.

The Look of Things

I gaze at the mountains—their green
the green of my strength,
their white my spirit's white, reaching
from death to the clarity of morning.

This is the dialogue I want:
language that answers itself—
as with the sky, to behold
and to be beheld.

II

A Message from My Uncle Felix, a Hunchback,
Passing an Apartment House in Greenwich Village
Where He Lived in the Nineteen Thirties

I strain along the sidewalk, dragging myself
from the hole of the subway
to the hole of my house.

These firemen lounging
in the open doors of the firehouse
gauge me with their careful distant eyes
like a collapse in a blazing house.

They do not know that I am one with them
in my vanity, longing upward
toward ladders and exploits.

I am for them the dense improbable horror
they can never quite believe in—
their secret deformity, their
monster from a fairy tale.

Here on this street—
a splash of night clubs, gift shops, sex shops,
sausage and pizza vendors, restaurants and bars—
all the equipment of pleasure—
this street where, forty years ago, I lived
under the shadow scars of elevated tracks—
what has it got to show for happiness,
this street of the young and the washed up?

A crazy sadness drags its eyes
in the pavement's filth.
I'm surprised to see two lovers
meet on the corner,
their arms around each other,
unabashed as actors.

Late November Woods

The trees give off a dangerous silence.
In solitude. Exposed. Confronting winter.
The sun sinks. The cold
drives deeper into the air, like a nail.

I am out of all the world's doors.
The blue jays rifle past; they are at home here,
in charge of things.
My life seems counterfeit, a forged check.

Back in my car again, I drive with relief
to the city's glass, street hustlers and
smoldering gypsy warmth.
I'm wrapped in the enameled confidence
of a crowd. I mingle comfortably,
braced in my con man's smile.

On Lexington Avenue

What I like is smell,
the deep beef smell of broiling hamburger
taking over the street,
spreading its animal strength within
this tunnel of stinging gasoline.

It knocks me off the long day's pedestal
of abstraction—odorless
daydreams in offices—

To teach me again
the enormous kindness of sensation—
for after all what is
the smell of a good intention
or of grief?

The Shirt

The freshness of my shirt this morning
straightens me up:
its urbane gloss and pride
a fabric of myself,
another identity pulled from a sleeve.

Appearances waken me:
a cool sun slides on the plaster walls;
the windows open on trees,
men moving in the street to work;
clouds bloom in the marble distance.
The sky without an identity bursts upward.

We stumble through common dreams,
defended in these walls,
hidden in light and light,
the mystery of surfaces
opening like the sea's silk
fresh beginnings in which I dress myself.

Opportunity

Opportunity I love you
Windows and watermelons march down the street
The air is nobody

Sky is in position
I am ready to endure my freedom

A riderless horse on a saffron plain
A lake that spins
A tree that lets the wind decide

Plums

Their excellencies the plums
plumped into dignity
announce themselves

Your amiable servants
the plums with their hats off
persuasive in their glowing skins

declare their readiness
to sing on your teeth.
Enclosed in flesh, in vests of sanity

juicy insinuations proclaim themselves—
The yes, the yes of the surprised senses
burst from a stone

A wintering sensation kept
alive in its depths
A stubborn magnified ideal of itself.

In 1938

Bickerstaff ate the school's free lunch:
watery soup with carrots, white bread,
apple, half-pint bottle of milk.
Public food on greasy trays
he ate in silence.

Charity that he had to take
like a badly fitting sweater.
It belonged to his Bickerstaff being—
thin-boned, sallow, dust-poor.

I remember him among weedy alleys
and secretive wooden houses,
hair so blond it was almost the color of light
above the pointed bones of his face.
In worn-out corduroy knickers
and hopeless sneakers
he walked the broken pavements of our street.

Chalk

Below the fire escapes
the boy with the cracked skull
spreads like a flower.

Were we happy then? Were we happy,
ballplayers in the hospital anteroom
staring as a coffin black as curbstones
drags up the last sudden love
of the stranger father
flinging his body over it?

Later, I bend my head
near his house, thinking—
the body is rotting now
beneath sunlight—It's still morning?
The chalk-marked pavement waits
for the game to resume.

Tugboat

Bright on the dark
drifting ashes of January. . .
head lifted back,
a fist of diesel confidence. . .
spray slung up, snubbed bow
slamming the waves, the icy slack
at the river's mouth,

your power grows
around a crazy idea of its own
unruly possibilities in the
careening water, you
with your heart of flame, your energy
like a belief in yourself.

Winter Loafing

I leave work early, out of step
with the rhythm of these office buildings
gathering steam until they could burst,
their glass hands clapping against the sky.

I drift downstairs with the snow.
Outside, the trees uphold the rhythm
of space and seasons—
black indications of long rests
in a movement of silence. The lights go on
as secretively as the tuning of a harp.

I guess I'm afraid of my death,
of missing out,
of never being able to taste the fruit of idleness,
and so I stand on corners, stand and look
that the day may not die,
and see the people pour from the office buildings
in a dark bright stream,
and the sun
like an old man's pink face, like a rose among graves.

III

Sousa

I like John Philip Sousa.
His face is shiny and creased
like his bandmaster's uniform.
They have walked on his mind
in a hundred thousand parades.
He never takes it personally.

He tells them where to go:
the bugles, the needling flutes, and drums
pounding against the noon of clarinets,
trombones that bray the pleasures
of war—those thrills

of a past you joyously invent,
funny music, finding its struts and swaggers
in our goose-stepping bloodstreams,
the enemy always with tricky eyes,
downright wrongheadedness and make-believe teeth.

Tell them where to get off
John Philip Sousa
forever and ever.

Job

Who knows what this One will be up to next?
Better to wait quiet and patient
while He drowns three schoolboys in a sailboat,
sets fire to a row of tenements,
and pushes clouds beyond a dying farm.

Actually I would like to groan and weep and understand
        this fellow
but even a sob sounds like laughter to Him
for He thinks He's only playing
and like a drunk at a party
He likes everyone.

Boys Playing Frisbee

For Timothy Pitt

You know the obedience
of your body like a lover.
Nothing you do makes a fool of you.
The disk lets you do anything—
it floats—
it dreams in the wind.

Like a lizard's tongue, you snap it
from the golden air.
You laugh with your wrists.
You shine.
You dare to glide through unfamiliar dances,
and move as only the best can,
only the naturals.

Elegy for My Father

I remember the feel of a hammer—
its grainy handle placing
its head's steel weight in your palm,
or the rung of a ladder
pressing confidently into your foot,
or how the sun felt on your skin, or cold water
as it dissolved the wall of salt
at the back of your throat.

I remember how you sang in your stone shoes
light-voiced as dusk or feathers,
how your shoes turned outward again—
as they used to when you walked—
when you lay in your dead body on the floor
and showed us the shining nail-heads
around each earth-scuffed leather sole.

The Sea

It will drift and ramble.
It will finger at the edges of the cliffs.
It will poke into the edges of the land.
It will drift as though to avoid answers.
It will cover and conceal its own turmoil.

It will come up over the edges
and again there will be green slime among the cliffs
and shells singing along the beaches
and a murmur among the grasses at the edges of the land
and water stirring among the grasses.

Long after the skulls of cities have decayed
the sea will drift among the grasses.

The Night

In pain, the body
turns without memories,
grieving in darkness
at the perfect designs
of organs, like stars—
impenitent, unstained—
until the mind is caught,
must turn to meet a stranger's
bloodshot eyes and grinning gums,
and swim with him
in a perversion that is itself
both love
and the sun darkened with waste.

The Youth Ghost

Glimpsed at the ends of vaguely familiar
streets, he resembles me, I catch him
loitering in crowds that seem
to possess him, push him under their flow—
he flashes out of it,
nimbly keeping himself intact.

Coming on him quickly, I'm startled
seeing his pants too short, his hat
that doesn't come all the way down—
all his clothes worn-out,
his eyes inhabiting dream landscapes;
detailed adventures on maps without night.

He goes without speaking, leaving me
amazed he could survive so well without me,
thriving in refusal to release himself
from books, fields, pavements,
or the melody of houses where I left him,
or occupied with climbing trees and laughter,
the smells of gasoline and barns,
and the long inviting unpredictable roads.

In a Churchyard

I study moss-green tilted gravestones.
I finger their names, dates and worn words
and watch them pace through time, like clouds,
when, miles away, they find my father

dead on the bathroom floor.
My wife blows her breath into his blue mouth,
she pounds his chest. . .

Where was I then?—so out of it, miles
away, so out of it, like a fussy rector
dabbling with gravestones.
They seemed to skip like flies between generations.

Flogging the Czar

What is the price of Experience? do men buy it for a song?
Or wisdom for a dance in the street? No, it is bought with the price
Of all that a man hath, his house, his wife, his children.
Wisdom is sold in the desolate market where none come to buy,
And in the wither'd field where the farmer plows for bread in vain.

—William Blake: *The Four Zoas*

I

Machines

Most beautiful when they're turned off,
with scales of dirt on them, with our lives
all over them—derricks
hanging over the Passaic River
at rest in the smoke-dimmed sun
like rust-colored washerwomen. . .
the light clean airplanes parked at Teterboro
aimed at a speck of sky to disappear in. . .
the white-decked grain ships at Welland Canal
rising or falling in the locks. . .

They make me realize something beautiful about *us*
we're going to die for. I want to forget
missiles sweating in their silos,
the poisons near Niagara, the scream of mills.
I think of men in the backwoods
of Putnam County—how crushed and lined they are
after only a few years—
how they love rifles, outboard engines,
can openers, old pickup trucks. . .
extensions of us, carnal and beautiful
things we'll die for.

The Ruler

Measured at school, lined up
against the gymnasium wall, or before that
the power of dimes and marbles—or later:
locker room comparisons, ball scores,
test grades—and finally: checkbooks,
taxes, horsepower, serial numbers, etc.

How did all these accountants
crash the party of the glands,
and build their second skeleton inside me?
I want to disorganize my life.
I want my days unmeasurable.

Maybe the careful weighing at my birth,
the morning I learned to tell time
from a clock in a Chinese laundry,
counted cracks in the pavement, or felt
the ruler's pressure on my head—
like the flat of the sword on a knight's
shoulder—were signifying moments,
saying to me as all of me listened,
"This is what is most important about you:
your length on earth, your shadow
a measurable thing."

A Photograph of My Grandmother at Nineteen

She is taken in the glow of mahogany
and silver, in the embrace of oak,
her lace dress buttoned to the chin,
her brown hair falling straight. . .

It pleases me she was once desirable,
not what I knew—a mat of wrinkles,
scraggled hair, thin-lipped
pillowings in a cancer hospital
. . .shrunken Grandma—soft speech,
bones and whiteness.

Ignorant, I took that ghost for her,
I gave her no right to be young,
ripe for marriage with some well-to-do bachelor,
a match for any of them with her brains
and childbearing body.

For the first time, I'm sorry for her,
seeing her young, all promise. . .
no poverty yet, no daughter
killing herself, no husband
dead three decades.

She goes on living in the vast amnesia
of trees, stones, wildflowers,
in my own fears, in humility and stubborn

fists and Bronx sidewalks and bits of grass
that remember no one,
in the dining room clamor of the family,
the table never large enough.

The Automat

Machines began to do the eating,
with bigger mouths.
Once, it was like eating in the subway;
yet something was magical in those huge rooms
—chrome, bright acres of tile and marble,
three-decker sandwiches on thick white plates,
food coming out of the walls

in little windows opened by nickels,
a dream of the future
when no one would have to do anything
but drink hot chocolate or roam in cars
around an electric countryside.
Machines would serve mankind
with almost human pleasure.

They're all gone now, Automats,
and the illusions of the 1939 World's Fair.

A Sepia Photograph of My Grandfather

He's sitting on cushions in the middle of Asia
wearing a turban, a hookah near him
and a scimitar.
             From Lodz, a textile merchant,
he traveled like a Phoenician,
buying cotton in Bokhara, Galveston, or Egypt.

It seems miraculous how they went everywhere
like English milords—those Jews
walking the thinnest silver line
of toleration.
             To escape the pogroms,
he sold his factory and his house
and slipped across the border with his family—
from Poland to Germany, my mother
hidden in a clothes trunk—
and then to England, where his business failed,
at last America—penniless,
used up, his name changed.

Here, in this faded card, still young,
he's playing out the charade of his adventure—
that short half-century of freedom
between ghetto and holocaust.
As if he knew it would end in human smoke
he took, reluctantly, that wandering step

to find another country, another street
where they could put their bundles down,
light candles, bake their bread
and spread the cloth for their festivals.

Diaspora

1

Even the grass should know our legends,
green in spring outside
the lion-colored walls, the rooted houses
down on their knees with age.

We never leave that old land
beating the sun back with its rock-
strewn hillsides, its sheep,
its dust of secrets. . .

Others can live and die like leaves,
can lie down easy as grass and sleep,
while the Jew
tosses on boards or silk, and remembers
tall thin ghetto houses, food stalls
lining a sewer, mongrel villages
waiting for Cossacks.

2

We are in love with being ourselves,
a people whom death seeks out and can never finish,
a neck of suffering that never bends enough to die.

And shame. There is that canyon of shame
on streets where they beat you.
Anyone else has a country of blood and numbers,

a confidence you can never earn from banks
and stately houses, or learn from sacred books,
but have to pluck from the dreams
of your steel-eyed ghetto fathers,
gnawing your nourishment from the bones
of all their survivals.

And of course they're right, the goyim;
there is no homeland, there is only
skin, bones, muscles, entrails—
everyone alike.

That's why I go on whispering in exile.
      Shema Yisroel.

Part of an Argument

Oh I get it
sun, cafes, fruit stands, newspapers. . .
you don't want Jews to be wall-clinging mourners anymore.
You want us all to be microwave technicians,
plant geneticists, Sanskrit professors. . .
two dimensional and staunch as recruiting posters.

. . .Bathing suits, oranges, traffic, public relations experts
that won't let us have our weird, bent,
weeping and muttering grandparents in the house,
or the ones who didn't know how to survive
the outcry for victims, and their visions
of doom's black clothes in the closets,
their dark like raisins,
and the sour twilight of ghetto shops.

Let me have my lament, my darkness,
my cry so wonderful it has made tears break
from murderers' eyes. . .

Listen to me,
landscape architects, dockworkers, surfers, hotel developers. . .
you want me to be straight-backed and proud as my young
        grandfather
stepping down in 1890 on a free land.
I can't forget his freezing prayers before dawn,
his lies, his phony diseases, his game
doomed leaps at appearances and the big time;

a dandified success American driving his Ford,
and Vandyked Litvak Talmudist in his prayer shawl.
He was a wilderness to his sons. . .
A mystery,
our fervent temples clinging to the world.

My Hunchbacked Uncle

If you were art, we'd find you
howling with Breughel's beggars,
black zeroes for eyes and mouth,
but you were not blind, you saw them also.

Your blue eyes asked me:
"Why do I share their bed straw
and their stone pillows?
Where is the genius of my body hidden,
calling to me from under stone?"

Inconsolable,
you swallowed Marx, Freud, chemistry, languages.
Too late.
It was always too late for the body
inside you, the child
with bare legs kicking through air
from a swing in a green Polish yard.

The Bicycle

The bicycle disconsolate for decades
among used lumber in the garage rafters
lies embedded in its year—fifteen—
which I can never let go, which is
no litter of the past, but myself
on the rim of the horizon
when the walls of my father's house fell open
and I was outside, everywhere on my own.

Two Photographs

The family picnic in 1937:
my boy face grins into the sunlit Kodak,
with relatives forty years older or dead
looking pleasant forever
into my eyes—

and that other photograph in *Life*
of the Loyalist soldier
shot dead, falling sideways in Spain
his rifle mid-air at his knees
and the flag of his hair left blowing
where it had been.

Those details: the lifted hand,
the hair, the folding knees. . .
Even homesickness seems caught
in his falling.

How many times his life has been saved,
and mine, and my relatives
eating fruit on the lawn
that summer day. Our faces in a snapshot
call up the gallant in themselves
like dumb animals enduring only
the present. I try to hold

everything in that present,
because every day the impossible

seems more necessary, every day
idealism pulls at me—wanting too much
like that soldier—
one of my many defenders
one of my own lives
                  unhelmeted
with no insignia on his makeshift uniform,
his cartridge belt and his hair outlasting him,
the canteen floating at the former level
of his ribs, and his hand still lifted.

Flogging the Czar

*We have no army. We have a horde of slaves cowed by
discipline, ordered about by thieves and slave traders. . .*

—L. Tolstoy: *A Plan for the Reform of the Army* (1855)

I want to flog the Czar!
I want him dragged out of his silk
to make him feel the fear-flushed chill
of one who is led to flogging.

I want to paint on his soft back twenty centuries
of screams, the odors of pus and gangrene,
the death-smell of ashes buying
with the worthless currency of ashes
wheat fields and apple trees.

I want to celebrate the day
the people didn't forgive him,
returned the bullets to their guns,
the guns to their crucibles,
the crucibles to their clay,
the clay to its sleep.

II

February Morning Through My Kitchen Window

What can it tell me?—this raw,
unornamented back of an apartment house,
an inward face
with grime streaks struggling down.

And what can it tell me?—these rows
of bathroom windows like the dripping of faucets,
slow lights behind blind slats
of bedrooms assenting to morning,

And the complications of the rooftops,
planes and angles irreducible as bone—
what can it tell me?

They tell me death is plentiful
and everywhere, that all there is
is wall, table, gas-flame, bread. . .
things and their stubborn purposes.

Clayton

A ghost walks over the tracks
at Harmon's railroad yards
in slate-blue work clothes,
pale arms bloodless as steam,
a negative of coal they burned here
forty years ago.

If Clayton haunted anywhere it would be
this grimed brick locomotive shed—
twenty years of his sweat in concrete floors
and bright red handkerchiefs—
he would inhabit its vacancy like a bird call.

He lived above our garage in the 1930's
waiting out the Depression, paying rent
with handyman's work.
I remember the smell of his kitchen,
the oilclothed table, tin plates,
coffee, hand-rolled cigarettes.

Railroads were the line of escape,
the knot-hole across a continent.
Boxcars rolled through his one-track home town,
making shelves uneasy, shaking the widow's cups. . .
The ink-blot engine, elephant slow,
lumbering out of a wall of leaves;
the engineer on his throne, the brakeman
walking backward on the tops of cars,

wheels that could sever a body, the bruised
steel plates and damaged colors of
boxcars; Burlington, Lehigh, Wabash. . .
Clayton's mythology.

His blue eyes sharpened with flame
when those huge wheels rolled away from him.
"Power," they kept repeating, "Power,"
taking his breath and blood and lifting them
into the glamour of the horizon.

I think of his blue-veined arms, brick red in summer.
I think of his intelligent, defeated eyes.
I think of how he edged towards freedom,
wanting to be used like a nail, to give his body
to the engines of a giant company
bankrupt now.

Driving in a Storm

Rain stammers on the steel roof.
Wind, unable to touch us, mauls the trees.
We push through miles of its slaver

past trees which build only themselves
past drenched fields—cows and horses
trying to shrink their bodies
under dripping leaves.

What have I built with *my* hands
that can almost smile like wet steel
into the eyes of lightning,
or roll untrembling, bearing down
—thunder on thunder?

I live in shelters built
by the enormous hands of grandfathers
and great-grandfathers; their backaches,
tired eyes, brains that wanted
to cut rock, purl through timber.

All their victories bought me
this steel shell tunneling through rain.
But hard as they worked, the storms
worked harder: thunder building itself,

rain pouring into rain, rain drowning,
wind eating its own tail, cars'
water-disheveled windshields crazed
by oncoming headlights, bearing down.

Wall Street

Getting my bread
not poems
from these spit-thin streets

Searching out the grains for bread
among these cornices
these pigeon roosts
this stone of money dark Manhattan

The poem never leaves me out of itself

The poem recites me from sidewalks and windows
from cracks of sunlight over a city
foreign to me as Asia

I'm always being written
The poem calls down to me from glazed hand-lettered doors
the half-truths of my ambitions. . .
the years go forward on my hungers
like a narration.

Getting my bread
just that
eating it, fleshing out, decaying

Bread must be the poem that always exists
my body's meaning
moving me through hallways

past marble where spring is hidden
past rivers locked in wood

The secretive insistent meaning
of the elevators the clocks
the faces of clerks
the cop retired to his bank job
the desk the telephone
the window's question
"Why not get out of here?"
the white shirt
the numbers crawling across the walls
the poem

Getting my bread, the poem
can never deny me
its voice.

Morning at White Pond

The silence circles from my oars,
touching the shoreline's mass of hemlock
—boughs dipping to water.

I cast my long lines out
to pull the silence from water,
retrieve from wilderness
morning in back of the mania,

remembering ages of lull before my birth,
before ambition drilled
into my skull, and my name
and all its possessions were pounded in,
and my trail cut out of this green
unmotivated wilderness.

Life Insurance

The salesman comes at me—
expensive suit, a leopard's eyes,
soft-footed mastery of hunting.

And I delight in this
and like to run with him,
and step in opposing circles,
seeking the throat.

He doesn't want only money from me,
but a little more life to his days,
another day in which to feel
the power to overcome someone. . .

Not hungry, but afraid of boredom
—a life without events—
his paunch sags, his legs
grow heavier, and he smells
the small gray lizard of death. . .

We shake hands, neither of us
truly essential to the other's life—
having lost nothing from this
bloodless combat.

The Banjo

There is some demon turning me into an old man,
living like a tapeworm in my gut,
turning me into a snowman
of cleaned up fingernails and shaving cream,
while somewhere in the life I forgot to live
an old rapscallion banjo sleeps with dust.

I'd like to take that banjo to my job
and sit cross-legged, strum and strum
and wake those rigid people into dancing—
those white men so white their smiles are water,
those camouflaged men who cruise
around each other like soft battleships.

I'd like them to remember their bare feet,
the bite of dust and sun down country roads,
the face they forgot to desire
carved and wrinkled as a peach pit. . .

All of them nailed to their careers
like handles on boxes!
There is some other game for me,
another reality could walk in any time
and become the boss,
shouting Dance! Dance! Dance!
Dance through partitions!
Dance through stairwells, envelopes, telephones!

It's hard to know which life is sleep
or where the door is with my real name on it.

South African Gold Miner

(Witwattersrand, 1950)

His life abstract to me as the word
eternity, I'd have to extinguish
the fury in my eyes, deny the trees,
remove myself—like an animal—
from history's fabrications, forget the sun
and the bird that sings in the baobab tree. . .

I'd have to go down
into the nexus of the mine,
cage-lowered a mile below grass,
antelope, women, sky—the Transvaal Plain. . .

I'd have to work next to his sweat
to understand the ruins of his eyes,
their eloquence like coffins or dead stars. . .

I'd bring him out in one lunge
to plains-grass, women, sky, antelope,
and cover him with bracelets and rings
of gold, ancestral gold, and white plumes
torn from the bird that preens itself
over his landscape, singing.

Into My Dream

My mother limps home bleeding.
Like everyone, even the poor,
she had too much on her to be safe.
Somewhere a mugger ransacked her purse,
threw out keys and photographs,
kept the cash.

I've seen the slums—the trouble:
they've got too much on *us*.
It's no use raging.
Everything we lose is payment.
Their mothers also have bodies.

That night two black men walk into my dream
and sit on my lawn
and lean their elbows on my grass
and nothing I say moves them
or gets them out of there.

Segregated Railway Diner, 1946

I sat down in the colored section
in my sixteen-year-old's gesture.
He sat facing me in his life.

A thin smile licked his lips
and disappeared in the corners. Outside,
gray unpainted cabins, red clay yards
where black men and their calico women
watched the slick trains pass—

It buried me, that smile. It said
I didn't know enough to sit with him
in that lacerated corner.

He studied his plate when the captain came over,
M.P. face the color of butcher's meat—
rapping me on the shoulder with a heavy pencil,
arm grip steering me to my assigned seat.

The Chain Gang

Stripped to the waist,
hard-muscled, downcast, under the guns
of lounging guards, they are clearing a roadside
across a palmetto landscape.

I notice one blond boy swinging a pick,
broad-shouldered. His skin is smooth, bright, sweaty.
His upright body ripples
under the rigid fury of his face.

His bulging eyes fixed on the ground
can see mountains, the destiny
of his imagination he can never get to,
where he could rest, a lion
in the wilderness of his flesh.

I see the body with its own career of gestures—
its bright roads, its dark roads
apart, serene. . .

Men must be carved, apparently,
like slaughtered steers or pigs
to find the marble of their bones
innocent,
innocent after all
as the stones they break, or rain,
or the guards in cages of their white voices.

Trapped in one chained line,
one terrifying combination of arrangements,
driven to taste each other's flesh. . .

The body sings alone
among the earth's arrangements
ignorant of crimes or dreams
or the curious idea of justice.

Night Landing

Descent is over the sea,
a black mirror of black sky,
a dark grasp of nothing,
the coastline amber with electricity—
America burns all night.

Road lights, ganglia
of towns and shopping centers—
from the air tiny
outposts of desire:
the need to have comfort
of night lights, the need to have:
cars and intersections.

I know I'm gliding down
from light too intense,
like understanding darkness—
seeing the sea's black star
describe the word *alone*,
the land's small fires
spell *hunger*.

Shark

He pulls his jaws together,
tears and swallows. It makes no difference.

His mouth like a black moon,
he slaughters his way through the sea,
his mouth his only soul, his genius.
It makes no difference.

He must carry his need around,
he must cure his hunger,
he must trail his emptiness through the bloated water.

Who can find enough meat?

Who can float this bubble of want?

Who can fill this sea-bowelled mill of guts?
It makes no difference.

The sea is eating itself through him.
The sea keeps swallowing its fish through the bowels
                    of other fish.
The sea withdraws his life like a card from a deck.
It makes no difference.

III

Mozart

Anytime we want, he'll sing for us
an aria from *The Magic Flute*.
He walks up all our dark stairways
carrying his candle.

Bug-eyed, bewigged Mozart
inwardly gazing, inwardly singing to lift us
clear of sadness and disillusionment.
God, how the keys miss Mozart!

To be human was to be like a god!
He'd have carved his love songs
on the bark of trees. He'd have sung
without ink or keyboard.

On his deathbed, Mozart begged to hear
Papageno's bird-catcher's song.
He wanted the Clown to sing.
Even Mozart needed Mozart then.

At Congo Tires

The garage is filled with the clangor of wheelrims,
the curses of men bent over tires,
their crushed nails, grease-smeared overalls
and hands, their boots enclosing
a thousand miles of painful arches and caked sweat.
Dirt here has entered their skins forever
from roads like a ghostly network of flayed rubber.

I need my fingers up to the knuckles in dirt.
I need the bulging neck of the manager
bellowing through car windows.
I need the power of the machine that clasps
the tires with an easy spin on rims.

It will let me know how to lie on grass,
to understand the thousand faces of grass
straining away from my weight,
to grasp the one idea of life there—
to simply exist—green dynamite
in the solitude of green,
as if it were enough
to be real as things are.

The Instrument

I've seen the mahogany grow pale
under the huge shoulders of pianists,
the curved beams brace themselves.

Such an army, so many games of chess
on the infinity of the keyboard, so much
access and self-disclosure. . .

It's like climbing in a forest
formed by your own hands, or singing
with your armpits, groin and heels. . .
it's playing Mozart in the Amazon
to a naked wondering people.

Music—the world that might be,
and yet the world as it is. The heart
comes out of hiding, saying to us:
"Listen, you can say anything you want now.
Here is the instrument."

Learning To Mourn

I'm an inexperienced mourner
I don't even know how to begin
to cry out like that old man
wailing in the next hospital room—
oi vay, oi vay—his two sounds
beating against the wall.

He makes me squirm
but I get his message better than my own.
How can I free myself like him?
How can I know my place as he does,
know how little I am?
How can I mourn, the cheep of a trapped bird
crying out violent sorrow?

Old man, teach me.
Help me reach the bowels of my cry
and bring it up, coarse, rasping.
Teach me to be disgusting.
Help me to exile myself from all
the populations of eyes and ears.
Teach me to live in that country
where no one else is, where I can
bash to pieces my good breeding,
my priests and pillars
—no illusions, the *self* wiped out,
unable to see or hear or understand.

Old man—lying in your shit—
you've let the angel of death from your mouth.
One minute of your unforgiving protest
is like true song: reckless, fatal singing,
song that is not victorious, not even consoling,
merely a sound you have to make.

Phenomenal Men and Women

My eighty-year-old arthritic mother
angled like a used nail,
pushing her garden wheelbarrow. . .
my wife who would take my suffering
out of my soiled eyes into her own
clear green ones. . .my friend
in the South who saved my life,
dying now of Parkinson's disease,
who could repair the broken
bodies of coal miners. . .

My father said to me once
with sorrow that stunned me
"I'm a mediocre man."
I've argued with him silently
long past his death, having seen him
"rising to the occasion"
like the ascending saints with their toes
still pointing earthwards—
phenomenal how they rise
how we all rise.

Jazz Recording Session

A zoohouse of windbag birds, blowhards
suckling their strength in the warmup
—solo fragments, breaks, riffs. . .
each man kept to himself, drank coffee
from paper cups, cracked private jokes.

Given the beat for the quick
first number they came together
in one voice, a blast of concord—
nails, teeth, hair, skin, nerves, muscles,
straining to reach the throat of the melody
to touch

its concealed life
the final statement for everyone,
(as I listened in the control room,
hardly believing
there were streets outside like broken pianos)
as I heard
their brass alive shining brotherhood.

Evening

My mother sleeps in her chair.
Her magazine lies face down on the floor.
With her body, she tells me
everything that's happened to her—
her face is like torn-up earth,
her mouth hangs open, stuck
in the middle of a frightened question.

What can I answer—
the lies we tell when we're awake?
The play is over, it's tucked away
in the empty pockets of furniture
and silver boxes given by aunts.
Now, a bare stage stares under a light-bulb,
stripped to a matter of facts, agnostic
of passion or footsteps or names.

The Last Gift

An old man struggles up the aisle
of the dark theatre,
trying to get out fast.
With pain he moves one foot
in front of the other.

His wife follows close
behind him, saying over and over
"I'm going with you."

On the screen, a man
passionately kisses a woman;
her tongue explores his mouth.
The old man topples from step
to step, his wife's clinging
plagues him until he yells out
"Christ, leave me alone!"

It covers her like poison.
He is enraged by pain.
He can't stand dying alone.
He wants her burnt with him
on his funeral pyre.

My wife also tells me
"I'm going with you."

It will take all my strength
to free her at the end,
to stop her falling into the flame
already searching my body,
to keep its poison from spreading
over her, or its tongues
from gorging on her.

An Anniversary Gift

I want to give you flame, comfort
and total comprehension, the discovery
and capture of fire, our lives
in tapestry complex as the Bayeux,
or Bach.

That would be it, or closer to it.
That would be one sentence telling it all.
That would be a scarf you could wear
all year, all years.

You know my shoulder, its strength,
I want to make it into a token
like a Persian miniature—
a compressed world of flowers and blood,
passion, painstaking care
and unexpected wings.

Summer Solstice

Epithelial as snow-crust, the daylight
clings last to flakes of white clapboard
and grass in the open meadow.

Another year wanders off,
another year I haven't believed enough
in each day's sacred step

climbed slowly, an Aztec priest in black robes
taking a heart in my hands
that might be my own. . .

I've worshipped sun all my life.
It slinks away. I'll hunt it
in the winter intimacy of fire—

the light that is always young, the burning
that goes as far as it can within us,
shares everything with us
but the end of things.

Death

It is silent as a garden spider.
It hangs there, waiting patiently.
It has eaten everything and never grown bigger,
still the size of a thumbnail.
I know that I am the fat one.
Everything that has lived is on my side
—the quickness of birds and snakes,
the glowing eyes of horses at night,
even the voracious sea-slugs that eat
the still alive flesh of drowning bodies.
All of the dead are alive in me,
are ranged within me like an army.
They sing against you, little arachnid star,
against you, immobile hanging gut.

IV

Miss Alderman

By the high steel hospital bed
a thousand miles from anyone I knew,
she sat while I slept:
Miss Alderman, night duty student nurse
with auburn hair, blue eyes, a perfect body.

Sixteen, just inside girl hunger,
paralyzed, sleeping on my side,
I dreamt of her in my fever,
my spine like a broken chair
on one of their broken Southern porches.

Coming out of sick half-sleep, I found her
pressing my face with her parted lips.
Desire leaped in me, all my body
helpless to respond like a sack of gravel.
I could see her breast.
A warm deep wave of her carried me off.
She kissed me, fondled me; she cared enough
to want to give me
some of that which haunts me,
heals me, makes things right.

It haunts me now that only chance with her,
that tenderness
lost to me in some provincial Southern city,
a nurse still maybe, or a housewife.

139

I knew it was no more
than kindness
by the blank calm way
she fixed her hair at the mirror
and scraped her lipstick
with her fingernail
and buttoned her dress
afterwards.

In the Hospital

The sun can die like anyone,
splintered among shadows.
A clatter of purposes rises from the street.
Cries float up like corks.

Pain is bright,
and the heart, how easily it vanishes
in foam on the lips.

I dream of a dawn rising without birds,
a white sun striding over blind streets,
the shadows thick and dark.

I move among them, tracing
their indifferent forms, like clouds
with the accident of life.

A Cargo of Parrots

With words torn out of the mute
bloody-tongued—
"heartsick," "suffer,"
no longer casual syllables but groans
of their oldest meanings—

all others' grief seems light
—a full sailed sloop hauls off
the whole world's misery
like a cargo of parrots. . .

All those wings and noises!
Why can't that fat ship take to the air?
They say this being alone with pain
is common, living through it
while the world billows around you. . .
Tears are the language, tears
that cut me free like acetylene.

142

Paralyzed

Who am I to expect
immunity, not to feel
blows from the ceiling and walls,
flame-throwers at the window,
or sorrow's commonplaces?

Rows of books in my shelves
move away at dusk like a convoy
humming outbound, hopeful.
I need to join them,
to take an indeterminate journey,
to grasp the earth like rain,
to exist in the trees if I have to.

Not an easy thing
to break myself into enough pieces
to cling to everything,
or to think about the idea of God,
or the bodies of women.
No easy thing, "back to the wall,"
not to become stone.

Shakespeare

When I was bound by sickness to a ceiling, walls,
a scrap of deaf-mute sky in a window-frame—
you gave me back the earth;

when they were ten floors under my window
you helped me smell the rainy streets again
and feel the textures of steel and cloth and waves,
and hear the voices of men and women
speaking their guts out. . .

Even more than music you rescued me.
Your people packed my room like a marketplace:
Falstaff, words delicious to him as wine
or capon, mocked the clanking nobles,
Hotspur mounted a stallion of words,
Macbeth was dragged by words to lunacy,
Bolingbroke, dying of words in council,
finally spoke his need for his son's love.

I am in love with their voices—
no one too low for eloquence, too high for misery—
telling me all the news of England or Italy,
the loot of living, the inexhaustible
plenty that saves all of us.

Killing an Ant

I crushed an ant on my desk
and watched its six legs
tearing the air like oars
of a whaleboat hurled out of water. . .

I saw my own body straining
to escape death, to live forever.
I pressed my thumb once more
to the ant's black carapaced body;
its mandibles reached for my hand,
an almost brotherly gesture.

The Table

This table of polished wood
with slender currents running through it,
with its poise that stands in another corner of feeling
from my dreams and griefs,

upholds so much,
this wooden tortoise shell, this ox,
between bowls of soup and coffee
sleep and trees, upholds

the lines of this poem which seek
the quiet discourse from the bottom of things
in these close-linked, long-fibered tongues.

A Fire That Suddenly Wakens

I lay on concrete
in the burned out barn.
I felt the ruins
of sea-life that had died
and become limestone.
I felt the cold
marrow-silent depth of the sea,
deeper than the reach of words.
How it denied me.
How it threw the sun back into the sky.
How it looked down and down only.
How it centered on darkness:
the end of its traveling
back into stone.

It refuted happiness: the climb
through sunlit fields; the piano sonatas
taking strength from my fingers;
the smoothness of hair; the hypnotism
of water. The floor was all stone entrails
writhing towards a shape that still eluded it.
I felt the sand grains through my shirt,
ground up, slung, sifted into submission.
I lay there, a body that had lost everything
but the weight of its bones.

The sky looked in, a laughter
that began on the first serious day,
the birthday of anything that had to die.

I knew I would rise from the ground
at last, hardened by its refusal to let me enter.
Like a tree my fate still leaped in the air.
Like a kangaroo, like gravity
demanding another body, like an oar that—
pulled by water—pulls against it,
like a fire that suddenly wakens
after midnight, when the fire is out,
a lion with a red mouth leaping through
the crumbled body of a log,
the hollow fingertip of night,
the burned out center, bone cold.

The Invitation

It's wonderful—the blonde
comes out of the restaurant
and smiles. Could angels manage it?
—this dazzling come-on, this fire
splashed out of nowhere like the sun
on that fourth Creation day—
what a smile that was!

The Dance

This rooted sinuousness,
this slow arousing of the oak
and blacksnake, the attack of leaves,
leaves opening pink mouths:
it is the carnival of oaks and snakeblood,
earth's carnival, clod's *kermess*.

You want to go up in flames, coiling
the other body like a vine or serpent.

Deadly? The dance leans upward,
the earth pulls downward,
birth so close to death
they almost touch.

Your Name

I want my metaphor for you
life-sized, not diminutive—
not like grandfather's *kätzchen*
or my father's *chickadee*
for women who could crack
apples open with their hands.

Of course, the men tried to make them forget
the mops and galvanized washboards,
the stir and kneading of enormous meals,
and the humility of walking one step behind.
They wanted to recover the play of love.
"Rough winds do shake the darling buds of May."
They did.

My metaphor for you won't be a bird
or kitten, but an experience—
the soft late light of early summer,
every tree full of easygoing leaves,
and every species alive, abundant,
and we not worrying about darkness
or getting home.

Dawn

You lie on my bed at daybreak.
Your pale skin draws the faintest
light to itself like water.

How many dawns I waited!—
in childhood sleep, the years I lay awake
at war with my body—

to see you rise from my sleep all fresh,
like snow fallen overnight on dead grass
nailing my testament of sadness to a tree
for the wind to finish.

The White Birch

The white birch
storm-bent over the ground
like a torture victim—
for years an upright sliver
in our summer back yard—
drags down wires, will have to be
sawed up, stacked on the woodpile.

Deep in its grain
one straightest line of light
persists, one shining that was itself,
as yesterday its leaves were
eyes of the spirit.

Acknowledgments

Many of these poems, sometimes in different versions, were first published in *Abraxas, American Poetry Review, Confrontation, Croton Review, Cumberland Poetry Review, Halen Review, Ironwood, A Just God, Kavittra, Negative Capability, New Letters, Ohio Review, Ontario Review, Poetry Now, Poetry Pilot, Response, Slow Loris Reader, Transatlantic Review, Westigan Review*. "The Banjo" and "Recovery Room" appeared originally in *The New Yorker*.

Designed by Edith Allard
Editing and production: Mark Melnicove, Lisa Reece, and Devon Phillips
Printing (cover): John Pow Co., Boston, Massachussetts
Printing (text) and binding: Maple-Vail, Binghamton, New York